EARTHGAME

Hints for Mastering
the Greatest Game
in the Universe

ROCHELLE P. BARTHOLOMEW

Printed in the United States of America

First Printing, 2017

ISBN: 978-1-5356-0353-9

Contents

Preface

Many of us have been told that attaining any form of awakening takes years of rigorous practice and discipline. I don't believe this to be the case. I believe this is just a way for somebody to sell you something and make you feel small. In any moment, we each have the option to pull back the curtain on this particular reality, the one we have become so accustomed to, and take a peek at the supporting reality behind it, and into our true nature. I believe that this liberating option is our birthright, and not reserved exclusively for a select group or certain special beings.

My experiences have helped me understand that we can enter something called 'the field of pure consciousness' through meditation. Not only is it possible to experience this field, but I hope to show you that it is more doable than you might think. Touching the field of pure consciousness is an experience of unspeakable, blissful freedom and I am convinced it is very normal for us to move fluidly through it, and numerous other levels of consciousness, at will. To me this an essential and very refined form of freedom. It is something no one can take from you. You could literally be locked in a prison cell and still enjoy this level of freedom, traveling as you wished to other dimensions of experience and levels of awareness.

I have been a seeker all of my life, always asking questions about the meaning of life and humanity's place in the cosmos. You name it, I've probably tried it. A few years ago, I found myself with a guru in my life. I was not looking for a guru, but nevertheless, there he was, and thank goodness! His name is Anand Mehrotra, from Rishikesh, India, and he's the founder of Sattva Yoga. If there is any wisdom in this book, then there is a good chance it came to me through him.

Seekers have a tendency to put their guru on some kind of pedestal of almost holy perfection, and many gurus almost demand a type of worship. I've learned that the highest purpose of a guru is not to be some kind of god or king, but simply to love you and be a mirror, persistently reflecting your truest and most beautiful self back to you. The definition of the guru-student relationship I like the most is the one Anand uses: a relationship based on a "shared intention of liberation." A guru is a teacher. As with any great teacher, I think you also want a guru who remains themselves a student. If the guru relationship with Anand were based on a hierarchy, in which he was superior and those listening were inferior, it would have been impossible for me to listen to him. A "shared intention of liberation," on the other hand––that was something I could get behind, and it made me very curious and receptive to hearing what he has to say.

In Anand's presence, I unexpectedly received what some call satori experiences. Apparently these experiences are common when one is in the presence of an awakened being. It is not something they do to you; it is simply a byproduct of being in their presence - because their presence allows for expanded experiences. The beauty and profound meaning of satori experiences are nearly impossible to put into words. All descriptions seem only to add to the mental constructs that keep us from having these kinds of experiences in the first place. After a satori experience, you are left knowing that it was inaccurate to assume that the reality we normally see is the only reality – or even the primary one. You realize that all the suffering you have experienced was in fact, self-generated. Not pain, pain is just a part of living in the world, but 99% of the time suffering is something we bring on ourselves. You remember that you have never been a separate piece, or unloved, as you once felt. The only thing between us humans and this knowing is a strange, often violent overlay of a thick, sticky consciousness which we call "the world."

Think of me as a travel writer of sorts. I have only had short layovers in exotic realms, and returned to report on what I have seen. I've caught glimpses - moments - of indescribable beauty and freedom, just enough to know that there is way more to see. Based on my experiences, I can say with confidence that we humans have access to mysterious experiences when we sit still in one place. Many of you are experienced travelers, and this will sound very familiar to you. Others of you still have the ability to travel, but have temporarily forgotten how.

If this matrix we live in here on earth is in fact a big game we came to play, may you find some cheats and hints in this book which assist you towards mastering this most incredible of games, and may you hear something soon which sparks a deep memory of who you really are.

Best wishes, happy trails, and stay curious my friends!

Rochelle

Chapter 1

Earth: The Greatest Game in the Universe

"As above, so below, as within, so without,
as the universe, so the soul…"
–Hermes Trismegistus

I f you are like me, you may assume that baseball is the greatest game in the universe. Yet, as great as baseball is, I have come to suspect the presence of an even greater game in our midst. Earthgame is part theory and part perspective. It offers a perspective on life that is meant to uplift you and empower you. If you are open to it, it will inject your life with a profound sense of fun and adventure and it will show you the difference between being forceful and being powerful. As you read these pages, it will be very helpful if you allow your mind the chance to open to expanded ideas about the true nature of our existence.

In order to get a grasp on a game as huge as Earthgame, we will need to go into life's big questions and look for clues. I'll show you some of the clues I have found so far. I find them in anything from mainstream media to mythic tales. Science and technology point to some very helpful clues. I find clues in movies, watching comedians, studying languages, and listening to yogis living in the Himalayan Mountains. Many clues are hiding in plain sight. We just don't notice them until our consciousness adjusts. Very much the way our eyes adjust to the dark. Your consciousness will begin to adjust if you follow the few suggestions laid out in this small book.

Interestingly, the more I look, the more I find that many of these clues point back to the Himalayas. For example, it is widely known that Steve Jobs, co-founder of Apple Inc., traveled to northern India in the mid 1970s in search of what all seekers are in search of: the meaning of life, why we are here, and how we can do good in our lifetimes. Thus he participated in a wave of cultural influencers, including musicians, artists, filmmakers, writers, and other tech titans who would travel from the West to India seeking deeper meaning to a life in which religion was no longer an option.

Much of what we know about Steve and how Eastern philosophy influenced him comes from the biography written by Walter Isaacson. Even though Steve Jobs came away with mixed feelings about India, his philosophy about life, his vision for the role of technology in human development, and the mission of his business were influenced by yogic wisdom for the rest of his life.

Other lesser known sources in the Himalayas report that Steve Jobs visited yogis in northern India more than once. According to one particular yogi in the mountains, discussions based on how to know the Self and how to pass this wisdom to the masses were routine. Steve was looking for a way to awaken the divine in every single member of the human race. His vision was massive. Whether he himself was able to transcend ego or not is beside the point. The point is that he developed Apple devices with the intent of raising everyone's awareness. Thank you, Steve Jobs, for your beautiful vision.

On January 22, 1984, Apple Computer ran a masterpiece of an ad during Super Bowl XVIII. The ad was never run again on national television but has been called a watershed event in advertising. The commercial opens to a dystopian and drab industrial setting. Everything is dull and cold. Lines of people march as if in a drone-like trance. They stare vacantly at a giant screen filled with a blurry Big Brother-like figure telling the people to celebrate our "unification of thought." In sharp contrast comes a blonde female athlete in full color. She runs powerfully toward the big screen carrying a brass-headed sledgehammer. Even though she is being chased by officers in riot gear (referred to as thought police), she is unstoppable. She successfully hurls the hammer at the screen, destroying it as the people watching the screen are shocked out of their stupor.

According to the ad creators, Apple wanted their computers to be tools of empowerment. The woman athlete is a symbol for the new personal computer. Her actions represent how the everyman computer will wake up the masses. Somehow Steve Jobs had the vision in 1984 that if enough people had a grassroots e-bulletin board that could help them share messages, it would result in a force that would balance the political powers that be. It is staggering foresight if you remember that it would be another ten years before personal computers would help us access an Internet that would even begin to resemble what it is today.

The yogi in question is referred to as Majaraj ji (not to be confused with Maharishi Mahesh of Beatles fame). He claims to have discussed Steve's vision for his company with him on several occasions. Steve was intent on finding a way to awaken the masses through his devices. The Majaraj ji says that he and Steve discussed basic questions any realized being must answer for themselves, such as "Why am I here?" "Where am I going?" and "Who is the 'I' asking these questions?"

Steve Jobs's devices mimic human senses. They can hear (through the microphone), they can see (through the camera), they respond to touch (through the touchscreen), and they can locate themselves in space (both through GPS and because they know if they are right-side up or sideways, for example). One of his basic objectives was to get through to the real "I." Any master will tell you it is essential for your development to diminish the ego. The "I" in those questions, or the ego, eventually will have to surrender to the Self for individuals to advance. Which is why the small "i" was put at the beginning of the products' names. As the Majaraj ji says, it remains to be seen if Steve's devices have raised people's awareness to higher chakras or if they have pushed people's awareness down to lower chakras. At present it seems to be a mixed result, but time will tell.

High in the Himalayas, there is a little town called Chaumasi with a modest ashram where Majaraj ji can often be found. His real name is Shri Girijanand Saraswati ji, or Majaraj ji for short. He joyfully claims to have received not only Steve Jobs in the ashram, but other influencers who may surprise you. For example, the creators of Star Wars visited him in the early 1970s and the intelligent power called "the Force" was the filmmaker's attempt at bringing down some of the advanced wisdom from the Himalayas and sharing it with the masses (also, some say the character Yoda is clearly based on the Majaraj ji, but that is a story for another time).

While not everyone will believe the Majaraj ji's claims of having had these conversations with Steve Jobs, I cannot see any reason he would make it up. He is not selling anything or even promoting himself. For that matter, good luck even finding him. It is possible to find him but it may not be easy. He is just there joyfully sharing his wisdom and meditating with all pilgrims and seekers who find their way to him.

What is not questioned is that Steve Jobs was influenced by at least one other famous yogi. Steve Jobs was known to read Autobiography of a Yogi once every year. Apple legend says it was the only book downloaded onto his iPhone and beautifully wrapped copies were given away at his memorial service, at his request. This seminal book was written by none other than Paramahansa Yogananda. What did Mr. Jobs find so important about this book? What do the yogis say about our existence here on earth, what happens after we die, or where we came from before we were born? The book is full of breathtaking wisdom but you will probably not get everything possible out of Autobiography of a Yogi the first time you read it. Like myself, presumably like Steve Jobs, and like countless others, you may find that it needs to be read multiple times, each reading opening the mind a little more, gradually allowing its layers and layers of wisdom to seep in.

Yogananda tells of the great yogi history which began many thousands of years ago. Like illuminated thought all over Europe, the science of Kriya Yoga was deeply suppressed and nearly lost to India during the medieval times. Eventually, Europe began enjoying its Renaissance while, unbeknownst to the rest of the world, the nearly lost tradition of Kriya Yoga was quietly resurfacing in remote caves of the Himalayan Mountains. As part of this new lineage of gurus, a liberated Master, Lahiri Mahasaya, initiated Yogananda to Kriya Yoga in 1893, when he was just a baby. Lahiri Mahasaya prophesied that Yogananda would go on to bring spiritual enlightenment to many around the world. "The message of yoga will encircle the globe and will aid in establishing the brotherhood of man," Lahiri Mahasaya foretold. Yogananda taught that beyond ritual and ideology, beyond dogma and religion, there is an internal path where each of us can connect with the sacred divinity dwelling within.

Each of us are on a journey and each of us are at different levels on that journey. We are more than this one experience. We are citizens of a great inter-dimensional cosmic play. Yogananda writes that the entire observable universe (that's everything we know of – the entirety of physical existence) hangs like a tiny basket off the bottom of the "huge luminous balloon of the astral plane." Let that one sink in for a minute. We try to feel our place in our vast galaxy or in the entire known (and unknown) universe only to find there is still more. Compared to the other realities out there, our universe is contained in but a "tiny basket."

According to Yogananda, after a soul has many sojourns (lifetimes) on earth, and is ready for the next level, our souls move on to the astral plane. In the astral plane, one can exist again for many lifetimes, but not in a physical body. Here you will be in your astral body, or "light-body." Yogananda writes that your astral body will resemble that of your youth in your previous earthly sojourn. There are unlimited dimensions and planets in the astral plane. You can see colors with the palms of your hands and taste with your eyelashes. If you want to go somewhere (or have something), all you have to do is think about it, and you instantaneously arrive (or the thing appears).

Lower levels of the astral plane exist in lower frequencies, and here lie beings we might call demons or dark entities who do not understand their relationship to life. According to Yogananda, these dark entities are caged in lower levels or "assigned to suitable vibratory quarters." Like all beings, over time, they eventually raise their frequency and are freed from the level in which they were bound. Many believe that when we sleep we naturally travel to the astral plane, but have to pass through lower levels, where we sometimes come across a demon or two. When we remember it in the morning we tend to brush it off as "just a bad dream." The fascinating mystery of existence continues to blossom in my imagination.

With my new awareness, the theory called "Earthgame" began to surface in my mind. What if within the mystery and beauty and unknown there was this little diversion for our ever-wandering and evolving souls? I mean, think about it: if we are eternal, multidimensional, and indestructible beings, as the Masters tell us we are, then what is seventy to a hundred years in a body? It would be not even a blip, a short diversion. Perhaps an informative, challenging, and entertaining game. What if earth were simply the most popular and best game in the universe? You know how sometimes you go into a movie theater and sit down and you become so completely absorbed in the movie that you forget you are still in a body in a seat in the theater? You are so absorbed in what is being projected onto the screen it's as if you are actually in the movie. Earthgame is like that. Although exponentially more absorbing, being that our senses and emotions seamlessly interface with the three-dimensional reality of life on earth.

Nick Bostrom, a philosophy professor at the University of Oxford, published a paper in 2003 positing that we may very well be living within a giant computer simulation created by our descendants. As far-fetched as that sounds initially, his ideas have been picked up by big research centers, including Stanford University and NASA's Jet Propulsion Lab. University researchers claim that it is theoretically possible to build a supercomputer simulator that could simulate small portions of the universe. NASA JPL researchers currently have supercomputers cranking away at double speed. Spokespersons from NASA report that inside of a decade, they will be able to compute an entire human life of eighty years. This simulation will include every thought conceived during that lifetime – in the span of a month. Wow! Imagine what humanity will learn about itself when it can run simulations like that.

Picture yourself riding a roller coaster. You climb into the car and strap yourself in; your best friend sits next to you. Your car is pulled up a giant slope as nervous anticipation builds. A moment of weightlessness as you round the peak and you're off. You go from feeling excited to terrified to exhilarated. You feel sick, you feel relieved, you scream, you laugh, you can't wait for it to be over, and you don't want it to ever end. When the ride concludes, the car pulls into the station, your hands still gripping the bar. Your hair is all crazy and windblown.

You turn to your best friend and the first thing you say is "Let's do that again!"

Could this be what a single lifetime in a time-bound body feels like to our unbound, timeless selves? To our eternal or indestructible selves, might playing a single round of Earthgame be akin to taking one of the most amazing rides in all of existence?

In Autobiography of a Yogi, Yogananda talks about a time when his guru came back (was resurrected?) from the dead by creating a "holographic projection" of himself in Yogananda's hotel room so they could briefly visit each other in physical spacetime. Utterly dumbfounded, Yogananda struggled to grasp how his beloved friend and teacher, who had died only a few days earlier, was again standing there in the flesh. So convincing was his projection that he could even touch his guru, his body animated and warm. Yogananda's guru, Sri Yukteswar Giri, reassured him that he was controlling his holographic projection so that he and Yogananda could have a talk. This is the chapter I recommend you not miss[1], because it is where Sri Yukteswar answers many

1 Chapter 43 of Autobiography of a Yogi

questions you've always wanted to ask a person who had just passed into death and returned.

This part of Yogananda's story sounds very similar to the story of Jesus's famous resurrection. Perhaps Jesus also created a holographic projection of himself, just as Yogananda's guru did? Yogi masters say that Jesus is what is called a "Mahavatar." In Sanskrit, maha = great, or master, and avatara = of divine descent (approximately). In the yogic context, an avatar is not a perfect being sent from some heavenly realm. An avatar has walked through the hardships and pain all human beings walk through. They are human beings who attained oneness with the divine while in a human body. They stand as helpers of humanity and examples of our own potential.

In the Earthgame analogy, a master avatar is a being who has completely transcended the matrix and the laws of nature and beat the game. Each lifetime on earth offers the opportunity to master another level of the game. The final mastery of Earthgame comes when one has achieved the ultimate freedom from karma, karma being simply our unfinished business and our unconscious patterns. Karma is like the glue of our seemingly endless desires binding us to ego-consciousness. When all karma (unfinished business and earthly desires) has been completed or is dissolved, then the true indestructible self attains ultimate levels of freedom.

Sri Yukteswar explains that a Master, free from mental and egoic constraints, may elect to come back to earth as a prophet (as Jesus did) to help bring humans into unity consciousness. Or a Master may choose to remain in the cosmos (as Sri Yukteswar chose to do) where he assumes some of the karmic burden of earth's inhabitants. In this way he assists humanity's evolution. It is said that the Buddha, Jesus of Nazareth, Sai Baba, Majavatar Babaj, Muhammad, Guru Nanak, Krishna, and other Masters love the earth and humanity so much that they have promised to stay with the earth, each in their own way, until all beings are free. This is where religions are right but is also where they are wrong: when they say their prophet is the only valid or true prophet.

Yogananda's book was published in 1946. The holographic method itself was then it its infancy. Wikipedia defines a hologram as "a photographic recording of a light field, rather than of an image formed by a lens, and it is used to display a fully three-dimensional image of the holographed subject." The holographic method was invented and developed by a Hungarian physicist, Dennis Gabor, who won the Nobel Prize in Physics in 1971. It is said Gabor pioneered his work on holograms in the late 1940s. By then, Yogananda's book was already in print. Obviously, Yogananda was aware of Gabor's work, but I wonder if it was Dennis Gabor who was influenced by Yogananda's ideas, thereby helping him to pioneer the new technology? At any rate, Yogananda left us a major clue for our technological age about how spacetime could be a multisensory and incredibly complex biochemical holographic projection. Perhaps the matrix (game) we live in was indeed created by our descendants, as professor Bostrom suggests?

Imagine you have waited in some kind of cosmic line to get a ticket for entry into Earthgame. You know you will feel afraid, you know you will feel alone, you know you will forget your true identity and everything you've ever known. You know your sensory body will interface in every way with the matrix, increasing the difficulty of disengaging with the game while you are in it. Finally you get to the front of the line (I'm assuming there would be a long line for a game this cool). It's your turn to slide down some kind of multidimensional birth canal through which you will enter a new flesh body. In the last moments you make oaths to yourself that this time you will wake up more quickly than you did the last time. This time you will remember who you are more quickly. This time you won't be so convinced by the fear and insecurity you will feel. This time you will remember to just allow the ride to happen and won't grip it so hard. You won't fall into the multitude of traps set by ego, and you will pay attention to the clues, and pick up the tools you will need. And off you go, another lifetime, another adventure, another chance to master the game…

I watch my sons play popular interactive fantasy video games with great curiosity. I can see the possibility that these games are rudimentary prototypes to the highly sophisticated games our descendants will create (have created, in the future?). What I envision these games have in common with Earthgame, primarily, is that they are fun and they are challenging, but I see more similarities. Video games take place in a virtual world. In video games, you are given an avatar (a computerized representation of yourself). You are given tools and weapons. The better games have communication and coordination with teammates. There is always some kind of mission to accomplish and someone or something attacking you. You have multiple lives. You find objects which make you weak and others which give you more power. Once you master a particular skill set, or complete a mission, you move on to another level, which is often a different world with a different avatar, even though it is the same YOU playing the game…sounding familiar?

In Earthgame, instead of a handheld controller, you have internal controls. In Earthgame you control your avatar by focusing your awareness and cultivating equanimity of the emotions. Where you put your focus or attention (free will) determines how your avatar (your flesh body) moves through the virtual world of spacetime. You master the game by piercing your consciousness through dense, absorbing, and convincing layers of 3D matter, and this takes practice. The ego must be tamed and put in its rightful, helpful place (more on that in Chapter 7).

Your avatar is your current physical body.

Your tools might be things like meditation, breathing practices, use of mantra, physical exercise. Anything which quiets the mind and helps us look beyond our conditioning.

Your teammates are your friends, wise teachers, and trusted family members.

Your weapons are your focus, your fierceness, courage to trust the natural unfolding of your life, and the guidance of your true self.

Your mission is to wake up before your avatar dies.

Ego and the collective mind are your attackers.

Things which weaken our avatars (use life):

fear

addiction to a perceived need for external power

addiction to numbing out, in all its forms

worrying

long held resentments

being judgmental of others

forcing and trying to control life and people

rigid belief systems

<u>Things which give our avatar more power (increase life):</u>

accessing states of flow

intimacy with the silent observer

breathing

any form of creativity

having fun

laughing

dancing

trusting the natural unfolding of your life

expressing kindness to any life form

finding a community

forgiving yourself and others

accepting yourself and others

connecting with others

and selfless service to the whole

A major program running in Earthgame (the matrix, Maya, etc…) is the fear of loss. This is another layer to the game which enhances its difficulty. Allow me to nerd out on *Star Wars* for a minute. *Star Wars* is one of many modern fables, and fables are meant to be instructive. The best fables have useful clues we can use in Earthgame. In *Star Wars*, it was the fear of losing his true love, Padme, which turned Anakin to the "dark side" (ego), rather than to the Jedi way of trusting "the force" (the unbound, indestructible self). When the Dark Lord offered Anakin a way to stop Padme from dying, he took it. The problem is, when we try to manipulate the laws of nature, when we try to control life, rather than trust life, there are always terrible consequences. This seems to be built into the game. In Anakin's case it meant he was indebted to the Dark Lord (also ego), and forced to carry out his bidding as Darth Vader in a painful mechanical body for the rest of his life.

If you are open to the idea of Earthgame though, then you will recognize that loss is only experienced while you are in the game. Emotions are only experienced when we are in a body, in fact Buddhism and other ancient teachings tell us the body and the emotions are the same thing, no distinction need be made. Now obviously, this world will break your heart in a million ways, and it's going to hurt like hell, no getting around it. The trick I think is in not getting too absorbed for too long in the hurt and the retelling of our sad stories. It is not in experiencing pain that we suffer, it is in getting *stuck* in the story about it for too long. The challenges and sadness we experience are meant to help us evolve and grow and feel connected to each other. We all have sad stories, but we can still enjoy the day, create, trust, love, and laugh.

The rules of entry into Earthgame are this. While in the game you will be stripped of your true identity – a complete memory wipe. It will feel like you are a completely separate being, separate from other individuals, and from your sustaining source. Helpful clues are strewn all about if you look for them, in songs and stories for example. The ego sets traps everywhere and they evolve as you get better at the game. All the while you will be swimming in the collective mind of the planet and will have to try to remember your mission while in what is possibly the most persuasive matrix in existence. You beat the game by remembering your true identity while still in your physical body and integrating or taming the ego, which frees the mind. At that point, the mind becomes very clear. It becomes a truly incredible tool and an important ally of your new state of independence.

Chapter 2

Duality: And Exposing the Matrix

"I think of contemporary bipartisan global conflicts
as a meaningless spectacle designed to distract
you from where power truthfully dwells."
–Sri Russell Brand

"Get over it, and accept the inarguable conclusion.
The universe is immaterial-mental and spiritual."
–R.C. Henry, Physics and Astronomy Professor
at Johns Hopkins University

The brilliant and simple Taoist symbol known as Yin-Yang references the essential dualistic nature of the physical universe. Just as the night turns into day and the day turns into night, there is an aspect of the opposite within the other which keeps everything flowing. The obvious ones: light and dark, life and death, male and female, sadness and happiness, inhalation and exhalation, disease and health, etc... These we are familiar with on the mundane level.

How about the physical realm and the non-physical or unseen realm? Almost every culture on the planet attempts to describe this ultimate duality. The Upanishads are a collection of texts central to Hinduism which focus primarily on explaining the true nature of life, the universe, and our relationship to it all. The Upanishads were written almost three thousand years ago, and some of the texts are understood to have sources reaching back perhaps thousands of years further into the past. What I find so fascinating is how similarly the ancient Upanishads and modern quantum physics describe the fundamental nature of our physical reality.

A basic premise of the ancient text is that we humans are not as substantial or material as we think we are. The Sanskrit word "Spanda," meaning "tremor" or "vibration," is used to describe the literal essence of all existence: a pulsating, dynamic creativity at the heart of everything. Quantum physics has String Theory which says that "all objects in our universe are composed of vibrating filaments (strings) and membranes (branes) of energy." Are they not saying the exact same thing?

The Upanishads discuss the existence of a particle so small it cannot be divided. This particle, which cannot be sensed through any human organ or seen by the naked eye, was called "amu." A primary characteristic of amu (atom?) was its inherent urge to combine (bond) with other amu, and thus build the substance of matter. How the heck were they understanding these concepts thousands of years ago without, accelerators, colliders, electron microscopes, and hadron beams?

To illuminate the point further, consider this gorgeous sutra from the *Vijnana Bhairava Tantra* written around 800 A.D., yet said to have been passed down through oral tradition for hundreds of generations before that.

> *What is this delightful Universe into which we find ourselves born?*
>
> *What is this mysterious awareness shimmering everywhere within it?*
>
> *What are these instinctive energies that undulate through our bodies, and move us into action?*

*Of this matter out of which our forms are
made, what are these dancing particles of condensed
radiance?*

Duality-pairs within the physical universe have
an aspect of the other within the opposite. A relatable
example of this is how when we are very happy, there will
be a tiny piece of us which feels sad because we know the
happiness is temporary. By the same token, literally the
same token, when we are very sad, we are united with
others who have suffered in the same way, this union with
humanity and opening of our compassionate heart brings a
sense of happiness, which will in turn lift our spirits again.
The Yin-Yang symbol is genius, in its simple representation
of this concept. It is said that the world literally exists due
to the inherent tension caused by two opposite conditions
existing at the same time. Said another way, the physical
universe is held together by the constant tension created
between two perpetually opposing forces. You could say
duality is the scaffolding which holds up the entire physical
universe.

Early Indian texts, especially the Upanishads, describe
the human experience as an interplay of "Purusha" (the

eternal and unchanging, consciousness) and "Prakrti (the temporary, changing material world, nature). Christianity might equate these concepts with Heaven and Earth. The Buddhist tradition calls this level of duality Maya and Nirvana. The literal translation of Maya is "illusion" and "magic." In early Vedic texts, Maya connotes "a magic show, an illusion where things appear to be present, but are not what they seem."

Here is a short list of duality word pairs from around the world:

Origin:	Our World:	Other Worlds:
Judeo-Christian	Earth	Heaven
Buddhist	Maya (the Illusion)	Nirvana
Hindu	The Material World	Brahman
Aboriginal	Country	Dreaming
Hawaiian	The Land	Mana
Contemporary	The Matrix	The Field
Quantum Physics	Spacetime Paradigm	Zero Point Field

So what is humanity's role living—as we do—between worlds? As I understand it, humans are designed to travel much more extensively than we might think. We are built for adventure and freedom. Are we not traveling into other dimensions when we sleep for example? Many ancient and indigenous cultures accepted a certain fluidity between this reality and others, much more easily than we do. One example of this are shamans. Shamans are people regarded as having access to and influence in the spirit world, and other dimensional spheres. Here is a short list of cultures who currently or traditionally accept shamans as an important part of their lives: Turkish, Mongolian, Balinese, Native African tribes, Native American tribes, Aboriginal, Maori, Siberian, Tibetan, Central China (Yuan and Qing Dynasties), Pre-Christian European, and of course those all across Central and South America. Such widespread practices intrigue the anthropologist in me.

Indigenous cultures believe that when we sleep, we literally journey outside this physical reality. They tend to put substantial meaning on dreams, recognizing them as messages from the spirit world. What is really happening when we dream? For all the study that has been done, sleep and dreams remain quite mysterious to Western science. (More on sleep in Chapter Five.)

One last thought on shamanism. Looking over the above list of cultures who have shamans makes me curious about why we don't have shamans in our modern Western culture? Well I did some poking around on the internet and I found something fascinating. I'm not going to go into it here, but I will leave you a breadcrumb so you can follow the trail if you are interested. I know this is going to sound crazy but if you Google any combination of these words: Santa Claus, Shaman, Magic Mushrooms- you will come across some fascinating theories. A word of caution, it may make you hope we start celebrating the end of December the way traditional cultures in Siberia and Mongolia do. You will be left with no doubt that our version of Santa Claus originated in that part of the world and you might start wondering if he serves as some kind of vestigial American shaman.

Chapter 3

Fear or Flow

"Fear is not real. The only place that fear can exist is in our thoughts of the future. It is a product of our imagination, causing us to fear things that do not at present and may not ever exist. That is near insanity. Do not misunderstand me, danger is very real, but fear is a choice."
–Will Smith, AFTER EARTH

"We can easily forgive a child who is afraid of the dark; the real tragedy of life is when men are afraid of the light."
–Plato

S o often I hear people say things like "I'm a worrier," or "I am an insecure person," or "I'm the type of person who gets depressed and anxious." When

I hear people make these statements as if there were something unique about those feelings I often think, "Well, welcome to the human race!" At the very root of being human lies a deep insecurity. When you feel insecure, unworthy, or inadequate try to remember how utterly common those feelings are. There is fear and insecurity literally woven into the human experience. There just is, and there is nothing wrong when you feel this way. It just means you have drifted away from a connection with your deeper essential nature.

Our feelings are likely our best guide in this realm. We are a species born into a dangerous realm with zero physical or emotional protection. Have you ever seen anything as vulnerable as a human infant? Infants are born utterly trusting and open, with no fangs, claws, spikes, or fur. Our tiny arm hairs might help us detect if a ladybug is crawling on us, but do absolutely nothing to keep us protected from the cold. The hairs we do have only help us *feel more*, not less. This too is curious, perhaps another clue. It would seem we are meant to feel everything in this body and in this realm. In fact, when I accept this as a likely truth, I feel unexpectedly calm. It seems we grow up learning to be afraid of feeling any kind of pain. Growing up I was terrified of pain. I feared it much more than death. Eventually I came to the conclusion that there is a limited amount of pain the body will let you feel before it knocks you out of consciousness—so I guess I can handle it. Since there is often little we can do to keep painful things from happening, making a decision to try just feeling whatever comes brings a sense of empowerment.

It would seem that we are not meant to live protected—with our hearts safely ensconced behind thick walls—but to live by feeling our gut instinct, and emotions. We have to *feel* to be engaged with our guidance system. Joseph Campbell said "follow your bliss." Perhaps our emotions help us detect the path which is right for each of us. If we feel inspired, joyful, optimistic, forgiving, loving, etc… we are probably on the right path. If we feel depressed, stressed, resentful, etc… is that our guidance system beeping to indicate a change in course is needed?

Assuming there is something wrong with us when we feel insecure, fearful, or have anxiety only compounds the problem. Have you ever had a feeling of inadequacy or shame and felt that you were the only person in the world who has ever had that feeling, and then tried to think your way out of the problem? I think I spent my entire twenties doing this, spiraling in angst about what was wrong with my life. Good Lord, what a waste of time! The mind can't solve problems of feeling insecure or reveal why something bad happened. The mind tries to approach it as if it were some kind of math problem. When the puzzle can't be solved, the mind just circles and spirals in the problem, and makes you feel worse and worse. You are officially off course.

I believe we feel insecure and unworthy when we become too disconnected from our indestructible or timeless self, but all we need to do is reconnect. Thinking something is wrong sends our minds off on an endless task of solving an unsolvable problem, which is another trap of the ego, and will keep you miserable, wanting, and waiting.

All the mental and intellectual efforts in the world can never help us overcome fear. The mind itself is involved in creating fear, so how can it ever free you from it? Talking about why we are afraid or insecure only keeps us locked in the reality (illusion) of fear. The ego will come in and start asking "why." The ego loves to ask "why." "I grew up privileged, in a good family, why am I unhappy?" "I am

a good person, why did this awful thing happen to me?"
"I'm so much smarter than that guy, why is he so much
wealthier than I am?"

Asking "why" keeps us out of the flow of our lives.
So many things in our day-to-day lives are a total pain
in the ass, but so what? There is nothing wrong with you
just because some crappy thing happened. Challenges and
pain and setbacks are an integral part of the game we came
here to play. These experiences are meant to make us more
interesting, wiser, and more compassionate. Don't let them
ruin your day. Feel the pain, cry your eyes out, and then
get back up and move on towards what you love. We can
always observe toddlers, if we forget how to do this; they
do it every day.

*"You don't need to know anything, everything you need to
know, you'll figure it out WHEN you need to know it. Even if
you miscalculate and make the wrong decision, you needed
to know that! I always say that pain is knowledge rushing
in to fill a gap. When you stub your toe on the foot of the
bed, that was a gap in knowledge and the pain is a lot of
information really quick. That's what pain is."*
–Sri Jerry Seinfeld

I recently met a Maori healer from New Zealand. He said this about pain: "Grief is like the wind. We are meant to let it overtake us and blow through us. We are not meant to contain it." This implies that grief is a separate energy, and something we interact with, rather than it being something that originates within us. Many Westerners have been taught the opposite, that grief comes from inside us and we should try to control it and not let it out. I think today we intuitively know how damaging this must be to our bodies.

I like the image of a flowing river as an analogy for living in freedom, or being in the flow. We've all experienced what it means to be "in the flow." Abraham Maslow called it having a "peak experience." Jim Fixx coined the term "runner's high." NBA coach Phil Jackson called it being "in the zone," and Miles Davis described it as being "in the pocket." Today, states of flow are being researched by organizations such as The Flow Genome Project in what they call a Flow Dojo. The Flow Genome Project experiments with induced states of flow and how those states enhance human performance.

Flow is a state where internal time slows down and action merges with awareness and the self disappears. The medical term for this state is "transient hypofrontality." This is essentially a Theta brain state (AKA the meditative state). When researchers study this, it doesn't matter if the subject is a professional surfer, a pro basketball player, or a seasoned monk in meditation, the brain state is the same. When in a flow state, your mind actually slows down. Your frontal cortex in fact goes somewhat offline.

We have all experienced the opposite of a flow state... which is panic. When intense thoughts rush in very quickly, leading to panic – the mind can barely function at all. Surprisingly, the mind appears to work best when it is running slowly. To use a computer analogy, it's a little like when you have too many browsers or tabs open on your desktop. Close them all except the one you are working on, and your computer functions more quickly and much cleaner.

There has been some research into Theta states or induced hypofrontality in the military. Using what is called transcranial direct current stimulation (TDCS) one study examined snipers in training. After TDCS, mastery of threat detection significantly increased. TDCS was also said to "significantly enhance learning" and test performance. TDCS has also been studied by the US Air Force to test for pilot abilities to identify threats. Again, it was found that TDCS not only accelerated learning, but pilot accuracy was sustained up to twice as long as in traditional training sessions. How much was learning enhanced in this study? By up to 250%. An increase in the potential speed of learning this large will likely bring into question the whole "10,000 hours to mastery" model.

As with panic, worry and anxiety are also opposites of flow states. The inner neurotic critic (our inner Woody Allen, as the Flow Genome guys call it) must reside in the pre-frontal cortex, because this is the part of the brain that goes offline when in states of flow. Worry and anxiety must speed up the brain past its optimal operating speed. When we are worried and anxious, we stop the flow, we try to control what is uncontrollable, and this makes us miserable. As one of my heroes, Laird Hamilton, writes in his book *Force of Nature:*

As long as you think that you're somehow in control of everything, you're always going to be struggling and striving. That's the opposite of letting things flow. Ask any martial arts master: The power isn't found in resistance. Strength comes from yielding to what is. Counter intuitive though it may be, fighting puts you in a weaker position.

Instead of trying to enjoy our lives more, or pursuing the idea of getting into the position someday of being able to enjoy our lives more – maybe we should just start enjoying! Right this moment. What if you dared to accept that much of what happens is out of your hands and trusted in life to unfold in a perfect way? Then you could sit back, look out at the horizon, and relax (142)

I for one am going to trust that Laird knows what he is talking about when it comes to accessing flow states. Laird estimates that his biggest ride was down the face of an eighty to one hundred foot high wave. One would have to be accessing peak performance, as with a flow state, not only to survive something like that, but to enjoy it enough to want to do it again! Characteristics of flow: it is a state of trust where we completely relax (we merge) into what is happening right now. The mind becomes calm yet highly alert. Flow states are blissful and bring out our peak performance on all levels. Correct decisions are made effortlessly and instantaneously. It is almost as if decisions are being made before or beyond the mind. The body moves and responds to the brain as one fluid, cohesive unit. Time is altered, somehow, so there seems to be plenty of time to calmly respond to whatever is coming. In flow states the mind becomes very clear. The yogi master would say the mind is becoming more like a crystal, reflecting pure light. In this state the mind is an incredible tool.

The next time you find yourself fighting the process of life – or asking yourself *why God?! why did this happen?!* – just notice how it affects your worry and anxiety levels. Asking "why" knocks us out of flow. When we fight the flow, we can get caught in eddies off to the side of the river, endlessly swirling and bobbing in tiny circles.

Here is where meditation comes in. Meditation, and a couple of techniques I am going to share with you, will help you to pull back the curtain on the things you worry about, the things which frighten you. Don't you want to take a peek at the Great and Almighty Wizard who flashes the lights and makes smoke come out of a terrifying face? Who distorts his voice through a microphone, saying mean, scary things just to keep control over us?[2] What if you do peek behind the curtain of what we call "the real world" and see that all along, it was just ego (The Wizard) making things seem scary? What if the physical reality of time and space really are God's cosmic motion picture, as Yogananda said? And what if this dear lifetime, with all its joys and dramas, is just one of countless roles we play out, until we master this realm and move on to have other adventures elsewhere? Doesn't that thought alone make life a little less scary?

Picture a middle school or high school age person you know and love (or picture yourself at that age). Think about how alone, fearful, and uncomfortable people at that age sometimes feel. Don't you want to just wrap your arms around them and tell them that there is nothing

2 *The Wizard of Oz*, when seen as an instructive fable, teaches us to see through the wizard (ego), dethroning him by discovering our own hearts, our own minds, and our own courage in what is a strange and wondrous realm.

wrong with them when they feel insecure! They feel fearful because they are alive. Wouldn't that at least take a couple of layers of anxiety off and allow the person to relax a little and think a little more clearly? At least they could be reassured that they are not weird for feeling badly, to the contrary. They are just feeling insecure, and so is everyone else they know, and it is all okay. Breathe. What if we could teach accessing states of flow to kids? If nothing else, it might lessen young people's need for numbing out. Obviously the most common options for 'numbing out' all have dangerous side effects, and over time, amplify feelings of isolation and despair. How amazing would it be if we could finally offer them another option? The possibilities for enjoyment and advancement are endless.

Chapter 4

Authenticity in a Mediocre Society

"Out beyond ideas of wrongdoing and right doing there is a field. I'll meet you there."
–Rumi

"If the world was perfect, it wouldn't be."
–Yogi Berra

Reportedly, there is a saying in India which goes "the only way to be liked by everyone, is to be dead." So good news, once we die, we will finally be liked by everyone (yay). For now, we have to deal with some people not liking us, without letting it change our authentic expression. One of the few sureties in life is that everything is constantly changing in some way. As we all know, this is good news and bad news. The things we treasure most in this lifetime will pass away, but by the same token, the most difficult things we experience will also pass.

Something which is changing or evolving cannot be perfect because it is moving. Perfection can only happen when something is inert or dead. Maybe a painting is perfect, or a rock is perfect, but something which is alive cannot be perfect. It is alive and therefore it is constantly evolving.

A marriage, for example can be beautiful as it evolves over many years, but marriage, like life, is not perfect. Even a long, beautiful marriage is a complete mess! It is a patchwork quilt of conflict and forgiveness and struggle and success and stagnation and evolution and joy and heartbreak and friendship and annoyance and love and a million other things. Even with all that, and BECAUSE of all that, a good marriage is imperfectly perfect. It is imperfect because it has movement and life. If it were perfectly perfect, it would be dead.

The invitation to move towards freedom is, in part, an invitation to accept all of life just as it is. Much of life is a complete disaster, and at the same time, it's completely fine. Trying to make life or other people something other than what they are will only make us miserable. It's our judgments and expectations which cause us stress and misery. This includes us as individuals. We are invited by life to accept ourselves as exactly right, just as we are at this moment in our evolution. As a mom, I can look at my boys as the incredible beings they are. It is easy for me to view them as absolutely perfect in their imperfection. They are growing, evolving in ever expanding complexity before my very eyes, and it is an exquisite process to watch unfold. We are not used to seeing ourselves, or most other people, in that light. Simply accepting things and people exactly as they are will immediately strip off layers of angst. You will instantly feel saner. Also if you read the chapter on violence, and you see how individuals play a role in the collective whole. It might help you to be a little less judgmental of the world as it is. If you've had any exposure with any twelve-step program, you will already be familiar with this higher truth. "Acceptance is the key," as they say.

I think we can all agree that society as a whole is mediocre. Society is a construct of the matrix, or maybe it is the matrix. Being cut off from authentic intelligence, society can be nothing else but mediocre. To be caught in the mainstream of society is to be caught in a race to the middle. Society produces so much banality that it is easy to become cynical about humanity. When we want to be accepted by a particular person, it is unadvised, but when we just want to be accepted by everyone, by society as a whole, it is kind of insane. Pulling back slightly from what we call society, we can see how absurd it is to want to be accepted. To be accepted by society means we have to snip-off those pesky parts of ourselves which might stand out. We risk ending up a bit bland and uninteresting. Even if you are celebrated by society, it will be short lived, and there will always be many who criticize you. Nevertheless, the desire to be liked and to fit in, to be cool, is a persuasive program running in the matrix. Or maybe it is just one of the challenges built into Earthgame to increase its difficulty. We judge others, while worrying about how they are judging us. How much time have you spent in your life swinging between these two polarities without even being aware you were in the trap? If you are at all like me, then I guess the answer is "can we please change the subject?"

Try to catch yourself in judgment of others and try to remember that society's opinion of you is irrelevant. When one person thinks you are amazing and another person thinks you are horrible, how could both people's opinions be correct? Opinions are constantly fluctuating, so to hang our sense of self-worth on other's opinions is like hitching your wagon to a paper horse. It is just not going to get you anywhere. Now obviously, it's going to hurt when someone says something critical but, if we try to please everyone, we might end up being quite bored with ourselves.

The hugely popular reality TV show *Survivor* is an interesting microcosm of our society and how it produces mediocrity. When I first watched it, I found the strategies interesting. The game itself is interesting, as is watching how people's different approaches play out. Unforeseen obstacles and rewards come into play. Physical challenges are won or lost, players are blindsided, alliances are created and broken up, etc…and everyone has to adapt quickly. I haven't studied this show as much as some people, but I've seen enough to notice a pattern. What I've noticed is that the people who win at *Survivor* are usually the most mediocre players. They are not the most or least attractive. They are not the smartest nor the dumbest. They tend to be likable enough, but not hugely charismatic. They fly under the radar for longer than most other players. Obviously, the smartest, best looking, most likable and most athletic players start to be voted off in the second half of the game, because other players want to get rid of them. That is *Survivor* strategy 101: set up your alliances and get rid of your biggest threats. The dumbest, most irritating, or those who are useless at challenges get voted off early, just for being annoying.

The best and the worst are eliminated and the last survivor is usually someone unremarkable in almost every way. No offense to past winners, as individuals, that is just what comes out as players of the game. The take away here is, obviously, who would want to win a game like this (except in the TV show where the winner takes one million dollars)? Why would we ever care what a mediocre society thinks of us? Especially when we are connected to our true identity: indestructible, beautiful, multidimensional, spacetime adventurers, highly trained systems busters, allies to the Great Mother, and all around fun-loving bad asses?

Chapter 5

DMT and the Pineal:
Your Own Personal Portal

"It's only gonna be about a matter of time,
before you get loose and start to lose your mind,
I told you leave your situations at the door,
go grab someone and get your ass on the dance floor!"
–Devi Mary J. Blige

S peaking of the clues left around Earthgame, it seems
to me that there might be something important
about the pineal gland. Why did Descartes call
the pineal the "principal seat of the soul?" Why are there
pinecones (after which the pineal gland is named) in
prominent places all over the Vatican? Also interesting
are the pinecones appearing on the tip of Osiris's staff in
ancient Egyptian carvings, and on the tip of Dionysus's
(Bacchus-Roman) staff in ancient Greek mythology. In

ancient Mexican archeology, the pinecone is held in the hand of the god called "Chicomceoatl." Assyrian palace carvings dating back to 713 BCE, depict four-winged God-like figures holding pinecones prominently in front of them. Depictions of Hindu deities are consistently shown holding a pinecone in outstretched hands. If you were to take a cross-section of a pine cone, it looks very much like the thousand-petaled lotus, which represents the third eye in the Hindu chakra system. Hmmmmm, am I alone in my curiosity here?

To Western medical understanding, the pineal gland is a small pinecone-shaped endocrine organ primarily responsible for controlling the hormones which determine sleeping, waking, and seasonal circadian rhythms. It is situated at the base of, and tucked between, the two frontal lobes and just above the Medulla and the Cerebellum. It sort of hovers in the center of the different sections of the brain yet, unlike the rest of the brain, the pineal is not isolated from the body by the blood-brain system. If you drew a line straight back from the center of the eyebrows (where the third eye is said to be) into the center of the brain, you would encounter the pineal gland. As it helps the body adjust its rhythms in response to light and dark, it is logical to conceive of this organ as somewhat of a vestigial eye. In fact, some reptiles' pineal glands still have actual rods and cones within them.

Rick Strassman, MD, a psychopharmacologist and author of *DMT: The Spirit Molecule*, studied the effects of synthetic DMT. In his research, he administered several hundred doses to volunteers in the early 1990s, while he was a professor of Psychology at the University of New Mexico. Vast similarities surfaced between what his volunteers reported experiencing, to what is reported by those who have had near-death experiences (NDE). Notable similarities are: a distinct sense of separating from your physical body, and, once separated, the presence of powerful, loving, and helpful beings. In documented accounts, recorded across the world and over many centuries, these are the two most common aspects of NDEs: a sense of leaving and looking down on your body, and an encounter with a deceased friend or family member who appears to be there to help you make your transition between worlds. When given synthetic DMT, Strassman's subjects similarly reported a distinct experience of separation from the body, and encountering large, seemingly important, and incredibly loving beings who offered messages of encouragement. The fact that these experiences are reported at all is evidence in and of itself of the existence of conscious realms beyond what we experience here on earth.

Dr. Strassman hypothesized that large amounts of DMT (Dimethyltryptamine) are released naturally by the pineal gland during heightened states of spiritual consciousness, such as birth, death, near-death experiences, and in moments of spontaneous mystical events (also called Kundalini, or Satori experiences). Skeptics say that these experiences are simply imaginings of perhaps an oxygen deprived brain. They say these accounts are not some sort of astral travel, but images the brain is creating exclusively within its own confines. That is possible, but what do you do with accounts like that of Dr. Eben Alexander who went into a week-long coma in 2008 due to a ferocious E. coli meningitis infection? While in the coma, continuous brain scans showed zero activity in his cortex (the part responsible for consciousness, thought, imagination, memory, etc.). Only the most primitive parts of his brain showed activity. When he recovered and was able to recount what he experienced, his near-death experience closely paralleled the thousands of documented NDEs recorded from all over the world and over hundreds and hundreds of years. He was able to tell the doctors details of conversations they'd had in distant parts of the hospital, which he would never have been able to hear, given where his body lay in the hospital. He met a beautiful young woman in a dress made of live butterflies in ever changing colors. She flew him over a landscape of otherworldly beauty. Six months after he recovered, he was sent a photo of a biological sister he had never met but who had died years earlier. Imagine his awe when he looked at the photo and recognized her as the woman he had met during his NDE. He also learned that she had always had a thing for butterflies. The fact that Alexander – who by the way is a Harvard neurosurgeon himself – recovered at all is astonishing, but what is most curious about his case is the fact that whatever he experienced…it definitely did *not* happen in his brain.

Dr. Strassman and many others believe that these experiences are not created in the brain at all but are actual experiences in other realms. They believe that the pineal gland has something to do with mystical experiences and it would not be inaccurate to think of it as some sort of portal. I do find it interesting that yogis (who come from a tradition which is at least five thousand years old and should not be casually dismissed) recommend rolling your eyes up, as if to look between the eyebrows to enhance meditation, AND how it is common for people to roll their eyes up at the moment of death. Could these be clues about activating the pineal gland and opening the portal for inter-dimensional travel?

Ayahuasca is a combination of plants containing DMT, which has been used for thousands of years by indigenous tribes in Amazonian Peru. Many Westerners travel there to take this brew and to be led by a shaman, and essentially to heal. The Peruvians say the spirit of the plant has always guided their people, even on how to make the brew. One Peruvian origin myth says that the people came from a distant star. Before they left to come to earth, their ancestors gave them the plant used to make Ayahuasca and told them to plant it in the ground when they arrived on earth. They went on to tell them to make a brew with the plant and drink it so that they could communicate with their family on that distant star. Sort of like a mulit-dimensional telephone.

Again, common experiences surface when people come back to tell the tale of their Ayahuasca trip. Many say it's like they were getting a heavy lesson from something far more intelligent than them, and were shown how deeply interconnected their existence was to the world, and to all of existence. Fans of Ayahuasca claim it completely cured them of anything from their twenty-year-long marijuana habit, to a traumatic, impacted experience from their childhood. What I find most intriguing about these stories, though, is a common thread of encountering someone called the *Spirit of the Vine*, or *Mother Ayahuasca*. She is said to be literally the soul and life of planet earth. Her business is the earth and everything to do with it, including us. She sometimes appears as an animal, before morphing into a feminine form, often with blue skin. I think in our country, we would simply call her Mother Nature (although for those of us from a certain generation, that term conjures a smile related to a ridiculous commercial for margarine from the 1970s). The descriptions I've read of Mother Ayahuasca almost make me want to face my fears of the jungle, drink that nasty brew, and meet her for myself. She will heal, although it will not always be a pleasant experience. She will answer any question posed to her, and there is a sense that she is reaching out to us whom she refers to as her children for our help.

I have heard people's stories. Mark Seelig is one man who tries to put into words the profound insights he had while with the Mother. After one of his journeys, this is the teaching he received:

The masculine world has become so starved for true feminine beauty and tenderness and has lost the way to be nourished by it. Always seeking but never finding it in glossy magazines and many other venues that sell women's bodies. The feminine, sourced by the earth herself, meant to be eternally caring, giving, and gentle, has somewhat lost the way to embody it. Really, the deepest thirst of the masculine is to be of service to the feminine, to protect and shield the loved ones, to go out into the world with a powerful vision and be lovingly welcomed back home, to adore and be blown away by the beauty of the feminine, to be fully and completely received and be nourished that way. Really, the deepest longing of the feminine is to be protected and held, to be cherished and adored, to

support the masculine in its visionary power, to
drink the heart-centered strength of the masculine
and be nourished that way."

Whoa, that one always leaves me a little breathless.
What a vision for male/female relationship. As an aside,
I agree wholeheartedly with those who say our political
leaders should be obliged to go through ten Ayahuasca
sessions before being admitted to office.

Another clue regarding our, perhaps dormant,
proclivity to travel extensively, is simply the fact that we
humans spend fully one third of our lives sleeping. I have
always found this so curious. What could be so necessary
about sleep that it outweighs the risks caused by us going
unconscious for eight hours each day? Science has turned
up little in the area of understanding the purpose of
sleep, or as to what dreams really are. The body gets the
same amount of rest by just lying down, so resting the
body doesn't explain why we need to sleep. It must have
something to do with the brain. Maybe the brain needs
chunks of time every day to process and download? Then
again, maybe sleep fulfills an even deeper need. Perhaps

it is the silent witness, our unbound, nonphysical self, who needs the body and brain to shut down so it can be restored in other realms? Many of our oldest cultures still in existence believe precisely this. To me, it is more evidence that it might be very natural for us to move with fluidity between worlds.

Typically when people return from a NDE they report feeling an immediate and absolute delight with being alive again. They commonly report feeling unconditional love and gratitude for everything and every person in their life, including everything in nature. They describe feeling intense and unavoidable gratitude just for being alive. And they often come back with messages they received on the other side from a loved one or a guide saying "you are okay where you are," and "you are always supported." I can imagine if, for any reason, you were to pop out of Earthgame temporarily, your friends (the ones who are not currently in the game with you) would be there to remind you and reassure you that you're just playing a game, it's all going to be fine, go back, finish the game, life on earth in a body is amazing, and you are okay.

Chapter 6

Violence: A Broader View

"The man who can reform himself, can reform the world."
–Yogananda

This section may be a little heavy, but we have to talk about it. We are all aware of the tragic and often sickening amounts of violence in the world. Mostly we sit by, feeling angry, fearful, helpless. What can one person do? Problems with violence everywhere are intractable and unending. We see so much violence in everyday media that we can become almost calloused to it. Maybe we can only take so much in? We watch events unfold in distant parts of the world and feel saddened, if not somewhat detached.

If a random shooting happened in your town, though, you would be in shock. The impact would be devastating. Now it is personal and real. When someone opens fire in an elementary school everyone feels the blow. Of course we want vengeance. We want someone to pay for an act so utterly inconceivable, something which should never, ever happen.

We start arguing over gun control, campus security, and government surveillance. We discuss new policies and protocol for identifying people at risk for committing another act like this. After a couple of months, the discussion largely dies down, and we move on from it. We hope it won't happen again. My question is: are we as removed from the violence in the world as we think?

If someone broke into your home and tried to hurt you and your family, most of us would probably have no problem hurting, or maybe even killing, that person to protect yourself and your family. I am not saying one should not protect oneself, it is a natural instinct. I am just saying that unless you have dedicated yourself to non-violence, almost all of us have that potential waiting within us. Given the right (or maybe I should say wrong) circumstances, we all have the potential for violence within us. Some say that if you have never committed a violent act, then you just haven't been put in the situation to bring it out. Remember that the next time you condemn a suicide bomber. I am not defending their actions, but it is too simplistic to say that they do those kinds of things because they are bad, crazy people. The circumstances they are dealing with are bad and crazy. Are you sure you would not do the same if you believed it would protect your friends and family?

Physical violence is easy to identify. Physical violence seems to manifests more commonly in the male form – probably because men are, in general, more physical. However, verbal violence can disguise itself in the form of mundane gossip and criticism. This kind of verbal violence seems to manifest more easily in the female form. Perhaps it is because women tend to be more verbal? Is it not a form of violence when we criticize, judge, and gossip? When we engage in this kind of behavior, can we honestly say that we are separate from the problems of violence on the planet?

I believe that every time we engage in this form of violence we are contributing to a level of consciousness on the planet which ALLOWS for terrible things to happen, such as a shooting in an elementary school or a suicide bombing. It seems to me that it is futile to try to separate ourselves from it entirely.

We cannot always control the thoughts which run through our minds – the mind is collective. Many of the thoughts you have in a given day are not even your own. We literally swim in the collective mind all the time. This is another reason to meditate. The practice of meditation allows us a chance to connect with our true unbound selves and to begin to feel the difference between your own authentic (I would say softer) thoughts, and the harsher thoughts from the collective that we run into all the time. While we cannot always control the thoughts which pop into our minds, we *can* control our actions. We *can* control what comes out of our mouths (ladies, I'm talking mostly about us).

Gossiping and judging can feel very satisfying, in the short run at least. It can be difficult to resist the temptation. Justifiable anger can feel good. Feeling superior can feel good – it is intoxicating in a way. If you agree that gossiping and ranting at our men are forms of violence, it is a natural step to want to curb our participation in it. We probably aren't going to be perfect at this but it is important to try to do better if you are interested in experiencing higher levels of freedom. Even if there is a chance it will help improve the world, then is it not worth the effort?

Chapter 7

Ego: And Why the World
Needs You to Meditate

"Mr. Duffy lived a short distance from his body."
–James Joyce, Dubliners

Being "political" is the ability to grasp a complex social context and adjust one's behavior to appear sincere, inspire trust, and be influential. The ego might be the best politician in the universe. What is essentially a defense mechanism gone rogue, the ego nevertheless has an important role to play during our existence here in time and space. In fact, it probably isn't even possible to adventure into time and space without one. It seems that the ego's job is to create a separate identity so that we can experience an individual life – a necessary constraint if you want to play Earthgame. If we merged with everything and never felt separate from anyone or anything else, life in this realm would probably be very confusing. Another handy task the ego performs is to make broad categories for simplifying the decision making process of every day life. When we encounter anything or anyone, the ego is there to quickly judge it and put it into a category. Useful, but a very two dimensional way to live one's entire life.

Problems with ego arise when it is allowed to become an overachiever. Ego was never meant to be the big boss. I think of ego as more of a low-level manager. It has certain jobs to do and tasks to perform, but that is all it was ever meant to do. In the current paradigm, though, ego has become the big boss.[3] We all grew up in this paradigm and have become used to it. Is there even a problem? That is a question we need to answer individually. To my understanding, ego is inherently anxious because it is utterly alone, it isn't attached to anything but your mind. It is separate by design to give us the illusion of being separate while we play Earthgame . If you want a break

3 Was there an actual fall from grace? A moment in human history when ego gained control of the human mind? Is this what the Biblical story of Adam and Eve is really telling us- they ate from the *Tree of Knowledge* and thereby left the Garden of Eden? Is the serpent actually the ego? For that matter is the story of Lucifer, originally God's (consciousness) right hand man- who wanted to exert his own will on humanity, telling this same story? Is Lucifer actually a personified and demonized metaphor for ego? What has caused more human suffering than ego? Is Lucifer not simply Christianity's branding of ego? More interestingly, was there an actual moment when the scale tipped in favor of giving the ego more power over the human heart? Was there a time when life on earth was more like a Garden of Eden?

sometimes from feeling insecure, anxious, self-doubting, worried, etc...then it is time to give your ego a demotion. Ego needs to be tamed, and assume its rightful place beneath the heart and the eternally kind, silent observer, which is also your true, timeless self. This is essentially the higher truth that every great teacher has ever tried to teach humanity.

In your mind's eye, picture for a moment that right in the center of your skull, just behind your eyes, there is a tiny captain's chair. Imagine that different aspects of yourself shift in and out of the captain's chair throughout your day. This one is telling you a story about how you are the best whistler in the world and you feel on top of the world. That one knows how to drive a car or make a spreadsheet. Later on, another aspect of yourself is telling a story about how you are the worst whistler in the world and you feel like a big looser, and so on. Whoever is sitting in the captain's chair has control of the "story" or "movie" you will experience. When ego is in the captain's chair, it will project essentially one movie; and it will always be somewhat threatening. The ego can only project fear, and frankly, that's a pretty lousy movie to be stuck in after a while.

Have you ever noticed, at work or in politics, what happens when a fool is given too much power? Usually this person, who knows they are in over their head, will compensate by being excessively authoritative. The situation is already out of control, because everyone, including the fool, knows this leader is not qualified for the job. By fool, I am not referring to someone lacking a certain type of intelligence, I am talking about someone with a lack of wisdom. There are many intelligent fools out there. People who's heads are filled with knowledge or data, but they are not wise because they are not connected to the source of true wisdom. The ego is like this person. In fact you could say that power, when it is *over another person*, is always false or egoic power—not authentic power. Authentic power has nothing to do with overpowering or oppressing another person. Authentic power is what we feel and receive when we are connected to our sustaining/animating source.

The ego may be intelligent, and may even have some good intentions, but the ego's actions will always end up being controlling, and eventually will be cruel in some way. As transformational comedian, Kyle Cease says, "If you said out loud to another person what your ego says to you inside your own head, you would at the very least be considered rude, if not a complete jackass, or outright insane." So do yourself, your ego, and everyone else around you a favor, and keep your ego out of the captain's chair whenever possible. The key to doing this is training the unruly, undisciplined mind, which is why we need to meditate every day.

Remember, ego can only tell us why we should be afraid, why we are fragile, impotent, and why people won't like us. It says things such as:

"why even try?"

"hide your true self because people will judge you."

"Be afraid!"

"You cannot trust anyone and you cannot trust life so you'll have to do everything yourself."

It tells us we will get hurt and that we will not survive the hurt. Ego paints a fairly terrifying picture. If you think about it, it is a tribute to the enduring human spirit that in the face of this cruel overlord and the certainty of death, we can still find the courage to laugh, and dance, and hope, and to love.

Many great teachers try to tell us that the greatest power and the truest wisdom in the universe lies within the essential nature of the human being. Once we accept this as fact, we can stop being seekers and start being discoverers. We don't have to seek love; we ARE love. You can never "find" love; you can only give love and you can only experience love. We can never "find" connection or fulfillment; we can only experience connection and fulfillment. The moment we start seeking anything, it makes us weak. The seeking itself is an act of weakness. All we need do is discover this great power which is always waiting, with the most extreme kindness and patience, at the most basic level of our being.

It is the energy of love that literally holds our molecules together. Love is the very fabric we swim through in each present moment. Remembering this truth has the potential to set us free from getting our asses perpetually kicked by the constant fearful fluctuations of the ego and the mind.

Imagine you are looking out your window on a calm, warm morning. You see the soft light of the sun start to shine through a clump of small flowers. An affectionate breeze moves the strands of the plant ever so slightly as they yield in ecstatic response. You can feel how these sweet little plants live in the exquisite bliss of the moment.

Utter trust, enjoyment, and presence. Loved by the sun, caressed by the air, hugged by the earth. Nature is forever in communion with the loving pulse of the universe. Nature exists in the field of pure consciousness, beyond the level of the mind. We can merge with the energy of nature, which is close to our true nature, any time we like. This is what *free will* means. There is no free will at the level of the mind. Within the realm of the mind there is duality, comparing, insecurity, and waiting. Free will is the choice to move freely between the mind and the layers of consciousness which lie beyond the mind.

That silent presence which is always within us is the key to our freedom. It does not exist in time. It does not exist in next week, or after you attend a retreat, get your finances in order, meet your true love, or loose ten lbs.; it only exists in each present moment. Spend time with that presence every day. Just sit with it and enjoy how life can open up. This presence is waiting for your company and your attention. We already know what if feels like to live disconnected from it. Would you like another helping of deep unworthiness, insecurity, and fear? That is always an option. Or would you like to try something else? If we can allow ourselves to experience the exquisite silent presence right now...then we are awake in this moment. Rumi calls our essential nature, our true silent self, "the one who was never born and never dies; it is silent when we speak, it speaks when we are silent." Don't wait. Do it now! We can all find this connection right now, moment by moment, and we all know how to reconnect.

My teacher is teaching me, as his teacher taught him, that if we let ego be in charge, we have only two choices: to be terrified, or to be numb. When on the unconscious path of the ego there are no other choices. Numbness or terror, don't you want to at least see what else there is? If you are not willing to accept those choices, or you are curious what else there is, then it is time to start your meditation practice.

In today's world having a practice is more important than perhaps in times past. If our brains are sophisticated transmitters/receivers, then meditation helps us turn the dial to find a station playing better music. If you do not tune a radio, all you will get is static. Today there is so much to stay distracted by, so much information, so many ways to mentally checkout, and so much static, that to be free—if freedom interests you—you need a daily practice.

Chapter 8

Meditate Every Day And Other Tips

I am going to give you the suggestion made to me by my teacher, plus a few of my own tips. First I'll just give you the steps I use so you can dive in without any further delay. In the second section, I'll describe the steps with more detail in case explanation is desired.

The primary suggestion is to meditate for thirty minutes in the morning and fifteen to twenty minutes in the evening, minimum. I like to more or less time my morning and evening sessions with the sunrise and sunset. If you are already meditating, this should not be difficult. If you are new to meditating, start out with twenty minutes in the morning for forty days. Then you should have no trouble moving to the minimum suggested amount of daily meditation.

THE BASIC STEPS:

Wake Up!
Set your alarm clock thirty to forty minutes earlier than you normally do.

Where to Sit:
Find a spot where you can sit comfortably. In the morning, face the direction of the sunrise (east) if possible. In the evening, face the direction of the sunset (west) whenever possible. When it is comfortable to do so, sit outside to meditate.

How to Sit:
Sit with your spine straight and your belly soft. Hips should be higher than knees for more comfort, which is why many people sit on a pillow or a chair.

Put time on hold:
Set a timer so you don't have to worry about going over your allotted time.

Primers:

Start with a breathing practice or a chanting practice for five to ten minutes before you begin your meditation. These work as primers, and will make settling in easier. I will suggest two and tell you exactly how to do them below.

Mudra:

Let your hands rest in your lap, palm facing up, one hand lying on top of the other. Or choose another mudra to your liking.

Music:

If you like music, put your headphones on.

Follow the Breath:

Close your eyes and start noticing your breath. The breath is always with the body, and the body is always in present time. Keep your mind preoccupied with breathing. This will give you a chance to unhook from your thoughts.

<u>Settling In:</u>

With eyes closed, pull your awareness slightly back and beneath (or behind and above) what you perceive as your mind, and observe your mind from that perspective (see notes below for more on this).

Rest into this place with a sensation of floating.

Feel into the softest, most gentle presence you can locate.

As mind and ego (storytelling) come in, gently fall back again without judgment or strain.

Keep shifting back into feeling state (which will be indescribably enjoyable but elusive) and away from thinking state.

Stay in this feeling state for longer and longer periods.

One way to stay consistent with your meditation practice is by taking it 40 days at a time. I have gone years meditating a few days here and then off for a few days. While it was better than nothing, I wasn't progressing. When I meditate every day, I quickly start noticing positive changes in myself. 40 days to make a change is just one of those recommendations that pop up all over the place. Yogis call this a sadhana. A sadhana is a daily spiritual practice. You start by committing to

a 40 day sadhana of meditation. One teacher told me
this. Let's say you start your sadhana and have been
meditating diligently every day for a few weeks. You
get to day 34, and for some reason you go through the
whole day and you go to sleep and you forget to meditate.
Guess what? You have to start all over again. The teacher
explained that you met up with internal resistance at that
point and since you did not push through, you have to go
back and do the whole thing over again to dissolve that
resistance. Expect to encounter inner resistance during
your 40 day sadhana. It may be that you just do not want
to meditate that day, at all. Or you may just find that you
are putting everything before your meditation. During
one of my sadhanas, I noticed that around day 20, I had
to really focus on my meditation practice. For a few days
it felt like my meditation practice was this foggy thing
I just could not remember. I had to concentrate very
hard to remember that I was doing a sadhana. It was like
I was walking through a fog bank. After a few days, I
was back to feeling normal and it was no longer difficult
to remember. Perhaps the resistance we encounter are
stubborn thought forms which are blocking the flow of

our lives in some way? I assure you, once you commit and once you know this, it helps you keep your promise to yourself. I highly recommend starting a 40 day meditation sadhana. You will not regret it. By the end you will have a new and positive habit and you will likely notice other positive changes in yourself happening effortlessly.

THE BASIC STEPS (in more detail):

<u>Wake Up!:</u>

I suggest you try waking up at 4:30 am. It takes twenty to thirty days to set up new habits, so you will have to try it for a few weeks before your body adjusts. (And by the way, this is just my opinion, so take it or leave it, but I say no snoozing! I think the snooze button is a stupid invention. You snooze, you lose. Enough said.) A few reasons in favor or waking up at 4:30 am:

• To challenge the status quo that everyone should wake up at 6:30 or 7:30, and that anything before that is difficult or strange.

- So you don't miss the exquisite show existence puts on for you every morning, in the form of the sunrise

- You will be more productive. Find out why the majority of CEOs wake up at 4:30 or earlier. You can meditate for thirty minutes, get a workout in, and clear your inbox before most people hit their first snooze button. Your mind is rested and clear, all is quiet and there are no interruptions. You will get more done in those two to three hours than many people will get done in their entire day.

- You will be healthier. Possibly the most dynamic area of research in medicine today has to do with studying pharmacological efficacy in relation to the body's internal clock. Researchers are understanding more and more how each organ has a window of time, within a twenty-four-hour cycle, when it is more dominant. Taking your prescription medications according to the body's internal clock can have dramatic effects on medicinal efficacy. Traditional Chinese medicine (TCM) has long understood the body clock. In TCM, your body starts its daily detoxifying/repair cycles (going through major organ

systems at two hour intervals) at around eleven pm.
It is best to be in deep sleep by then, which for most
people means getting to sleep between nine and ten
pm. If you are waking up at 4:30 am, you will probably
need to start going to sleep earlier, or you may notice
you are falling behind on sleep. Getting to sleep earlier
allows your body to go through its natural nightly
detox cycle more effectively.

- The early morning is a naturally contemplative time.
  This is the optimal time to meditate, set goals, or work
  on special projects that require extra creativity or
  concentration.

Primers:

Pranayama (breathing practices):

"Nadi Shodhana Pranayama" (which translates to
the drastically less poetic "alternate nostril control of
breath") The physical benefits of this breathing practice
are extensive. It is said to oxygenate the body, release
toxins through the respiratory system, reduce stress and
anxiety, enhance mental clarity and concentration, etc…
If you were going to pick one pranayama, this one would

probably give you the most bang for your buck. I suggest doing Nadi Shodhana Pranayama for about five minutes before you begin your meditation. It will help you settle in. Take your right hand and make the peace sign. Place the tips of your index and middle fingers between your eyebrows. Close your right nostril with your right thumb and slowly inhale through the left nostril. With full lungs, hold the breath, release the right nostril, and close your left nostril with your right pinky. Exhale slowly through the right nostril. Inhale slowly through right nostril. Hold your breath at the top of the breath and release the left nostril, while closing the right nostril with the thumb again. Exhale through the left nostril. Inhale slowly through the left nostril, and repeat for about three to five minutes. You will feel more calm and alert.

Mantra (sounds made to enhance meditation or concentration):

Chanting "OM." Another technique to try for about five minutes before you settle in for your meditation is chanting OM, or AUM. Mantra is a Sanskrit word which roughly translates to "sound tool." Some scholars say it comes from the root words man = "mind" + tria = "a liberating device."[4]

So mantra in this sense is a "mind liberating device." Sanskrit is one of the oldest known languages in the world, at least six thousand years old, and the primary sacred language of Hinduism. It is the mother tongue of many Indo-European languages, including Latin, English, German, French, Italian, Spanish, and most of what is spoken in India. *News & World Report HEALTH* published an article in 2013 entitled: "Your Brain on Om: The Science of Mantra." Basic sounds in the Sanskrit language (several of which are curiously absent in the English language) affect the mind and body in observable ways. Before the brain assigns meaning to a word, the initial seed sounds create resonance and interactions in different parts of the nervous system. The article goes on to say this:

---

4 I believe those who say intelligent use of mantra is a powerful and largely forgotten science. It is likely that what we think of as spells came from uninitiated exposure to mantra use. The gypsies in Europe came largely through Romania, they have a Romanian based language. They came into Romania from India around the year 500 AD. It seems very likely they brought Sanskrit mantra with them which were misunderstood by the medieval European mindset and thought of as being a type of magic. But they are not magic. They work on the subtle body and other esoteric energies which are not yet understood by western science. You don't have to believe in mantra, they work regardless of your beliefs. If you want to experiment, find a mantra that you are attracted to and say it in Sanskrit 108 times each day, for 40 days. See what you think after trying it.

The A (pronounced ä, as in "car") can feel like a wide opening, and has a broader vibratory effect on the physical body, approximating the gross consciousness of the waking state. The U (pronounced o̅o̅, as in "soup") has a funneling effect, narrowing the consciousness into subtler sensations, such as thoughts and impressions, approximating the dream state. The more nasal M sound is like the drone of a bee; it makes the cranium vibrate in a kind of undifferentiated and ubiquitous earthquake over the convolutions or valleys in the cerebral cortex, approximating the deep, dreamless sleep state of consciousness. Traditionally, Aum represents, and has the capacity to progressively open up the practitioner to, the ever-present formless and timeless reality, the background radiation of the cosmos that echoes the Big Bang."

Start by taking a deep, slow breath in through the nose. Without rushing, open with the 'Aaaah' sound, smoothly transition to the 'Uuuu' sound, and gradually end with lips gently closing to make the 'Mmmm' sound. With lips still closed, softly shorten the back of your throat to create the 'NG' sound near the end of each OM chant. The vibration this sound creates in the center of your head is said to stimulate and help clear the pineal gland.

Mudra:

Mudras are ancient hand positions or body positions used in yoga to stimulate different beneficial energies in the body. Some would call them part of a forgotten science. The common translation for mudra is "seal" or "lock," which involves the geometry and circuitry of the body. When thought of in terms of energy and electricity, one can envision how a mudra creates a closed circuit. A closed circuit simply allows a current to flow uninterrupted. We usually think of mudras which involve the hands, and these are the most common. There are whole-body mudras as well. In fact, every yoga asana (pose) is a body mudra designed to move the energies in the body in particular and beneficial ways. People spontaneously use mudras in everyday life (think of giving the 'thumbs up,' the shaka sign, or flipping someone off—these are popular mudras).

Anjali mudra, (or hands in prayer position) creates a closed circuit between the palms. It is believed to calm mental stress and anxiety, assisting one to focus and meditate. Used constantly by yoga teachers, gurus, and nuns, but also spontaneously by people pleading for assistance or mercy.

Hakini mudra is said to focus one's concentration and help with memory recall. Hakini mudra is created by touching all five fingertips lightly against the same fingers of the other hand. Palms are gently curved towards each other as if cupping an imaginary ball between the hands. Fingertips can be held gently together or lightly tapped against one another. Hakini mudra is very practical and may be used when you want to conjure a memory or detail from deep within your past, a person's name you forgot, or a fact you once learned and need to recall for an exam or when talking in front of people. Picture a CEO in a board room making an important point. He brings his hands in front of him, tapping the tips of the fingers on the right hand to the tips of the fingers on the left hand. Perhaps he is simply mimicking other CEOs who use this power gesture, or his subconscious mind knows it helps strengthen his mind and memory. Either way, he is using an ancient technique which yogis have understood for thousands of years.

Dhyana mudra is used to enhance meditation. Rest your left hand in your lap with the palm facing up. Place your right hand on top of the left with palm facing up. Technically you bring the tips of the thumbs touching. If you can do this and keep tension out of your arms and shoulders then go for it. If not, just allow thumbs to touch in any comfortable, easy way.

Music:

If you don't want music, don't use music. I mention it because it really helps me. If you want to use music, pick tracks that don't have words. The exception would be if the words are Sanskrit chants. Something with a drone or the tanpura is especially helpful. If you like, focus on the sound of the drone behind the music. Music is a good metaphor for the layers in our consciousness. A particular track could have the tanpura (drone), strings, flute, vocals, and so on. You can think of the strings and flutes like thoughts on the surface. The drone then is like the deeper experience with self. While listening at the level of the drone, you can still hear the other layers of music, but they are not what you are experiencing in that moment. Listen on this level, breathe, and relax some more.

Follow the Breath:

The breath is always in the body, and the body is always in present time. This is why so many yoga and meditation teachers guide you to focus on your breath. It is a simple and effective way to get yourself back into present time. I find it is helpful to breathe in and out softly and to focus on the air gently flowing in and out. When I focus on my breath, sometimes it feels like it is difficult to breathe. It can feel like I have to put effort into what is otherwise effortless, or it won't happen. I have found that if I just sit and observe this sensation for a while, it passes and breathing becomes effortless again. Sometimes people experience other strange sensations in meditation, like shaking, or a sensation of vibrating, etc.. Try to just stay with the presence of observing whatever is happening. As more prana (chi, ki, life-force energy) is coming into your body, it may feel strange at first. Trust that your body and your true self know what they are doing and try to stay relaxed and nonjudgmental.

Settling In:

As you sit down and close your eyes, bring your awareness to the backs or your eyes. Soften and relax. Breathe.

Bring your awareness to that space behind your heart. Let any tension spill off as you breathe into this gorgeous energy center.

Slide your attention down to your belly. Locate with your mind's eye, the center of your belly. Now expand soft ripples of relaxation out from this point in all directions.

Even as you start to experience blissful and expansive moments in your meditation, notice how the mind or ego wants to narrate what is happening. This is another way ego is trying to regain control. When you notice this happening gently feel your way back to the compassionate observer and to a deeper state of non-doing. Relax your mind more deeply.

It is impossible to stop the mind from creating thoughts. Don't even try. The idea is to "meet yourself before the mind." Remember the fish in the net analogy? Your awareness is the fish and your mind is the net. Imagine that you encounter the fish just before it enters the net. See if you can float in that space. This will be a feeling state – rather than a thinking state – because you have not entered the mental net. So the goal is different from trying to stop the mind from having thoughts. You are locating a level of experience which is far more refined than the realm of thoughts. From that alert and clear vantage, your thoughts will be like a distant murmur, not loud- as they usually are.

Let us say you have been meditating for fifteen days straight and you find yourself at the end of each session saying to yourself, "Dammit! I spent the whole time thinking again!" Don't worry, relax and stay with it. By setting the time aside, you are in your practice. You are probably closer than you think, to locating your access point.

Once you feel your way to your point of contact, you will know it. Practice letting yourself stay in union with your unbound self, the silent observer, for longer and longer periods of time. It feels amazing. In this way, become more familiar with the gentleness, kindness, and wisdom of this aspect of yourself. With a little time, this aspect will want to express itself more and more in other areas of your life.

Obviously, this will be good for you, and good for everyone around you.

Chapter 9

Split Awareness:
An Intermediate Practice

*"Imagine that what awakens in you has lived forever, and
that it wakes within a soft and resilient casing of tissue
that will take you wherever you want; that you have these
delicate surfaces through which to feel wind and see light
and sense the spirit of everything else that has ever lived.*

*Imagine that once awake you walk in a world where small
creatures fly about your head and sing, where colorful,
juicy things grow on trees, that you can eat what grows
from dirt. Imagine that there are others you can talk
with, laugh with and cry with. Others you can love.*

*Imagine that you can open your eyes and dance in a world
where water can fall from the sky, that you can open your
throat and song can come from it, that you can find the
sun and let it warm the flower of you into being.*

Now open your eyes and receive that it is all true,
it is all here, it is all now..."
–Mark Nepo, *The Book of Awakening*

"We are here through no particular merit of our
own but through the profound generosity
and kindness of existence itself."
–Anand Mehrotra

As I said in the previous chapter, meditating for thirty minutes in the morning and fifteen to twenty minutes in the evening is the minimum. Once you are meditating at least this much, you can start increasing your time. The benefits will only increase. Again, if you are new to meditating, start with twenty minutes each morning, and you can work up from there. My teacher, Anand, says that in today's world (which as we know, can be a bit intense) this is the minimum requirement for our bodies to become attuned to, and be able to hold a new frequency. When we sit in meditation, the supreme state of 'non-doing,' we are simply allowing ourselves to experience deeper states of awareness, which are always right there -waiting for us to arrive. It is like tuning a radio. The signals are always there, but if we don't turn the dial, we will only get static. Meditation is like turning the dial, and it will help you attune your apparatus. And then the music is just there, waiting. It is so kind and patient. Even if we are out of tune for a long time, the music is always just there, and the second we drop in, it will simply start playing.

If we don't practice with some degree of diligence and discipline, attaining freedom and peace could simply remain along a receding horizon. You might get stuck living continually on the level of the intellect only. Remember that learning about this is essential, but don't get stuck there. We have to start doing it. By the same token, try not to turn this suggested practice into another linear way to measure and judge yourself. This is just the ego coming in again. Remember, ego will turn any system into something dry and punishing if it is allowed to. That is all it knows. So instead of being rigid, be fierce. Mastering Earthgame requires your fierceness. This type of fierceness is referenced deep within the yogic tradition and the Hindu Pantheon, and many other traditions from all over the world.

Kali for example, the Hindu goddess of empowerment, is here to help us at this point in our development.

Sometimes Kali is described as a young and beautiful maiden with a gentle smile. She offers bounty and dispels fear with a wave of her right hand. But Kali means business and can also be downright scary. At other times she is shown with matted hair, bloodshot eyes, a sword in one hand and a severed dripping human head in the other; she wears more decapitated heads around her waist, and a garland of human skulls around her neck. She's clearly been through some shit. Her business is defeating the human mind and ego (as depicted by all the cut off heads and skulls). Kali is a bad ass, and luckily she is on your side (and by your side, I mean she is on the side of your true self). Kali sometimes appears standing on top of the demon known as Raktabija (blood seed). Wherever Raktabija is present on a battle field, each drop of blood spilled onto the earth creates a new demon. Kali is commonly shown with her tongue sticking out (as on the iconic Rolling Stones album cover). When she defeats Raktabija, she stretches her tongue over the entire earth, licking up each drop of blood, while devouring Raktabija and his duplicates into her gaping mouth. Kali just isn't putting up with any BS created by humans running around with their egos in charge. This path just ends in suffering and bloodshed, and it leaves a huge mess for her to clean up and we all know that extra messes, tend to put the ladies in a bad mood. The takeaway here is this; Kali promises that our efforts at a disciplined practice will bring success quickly. She will meet us more than half way. Commit to a daily practice, show some grit, and Kali will come to your aid—swiftly chopping off the metaphorical head of an overactive and tyrannical ego for you.

It is said she appears as the beautiful maiden to our true self and as the terrifying *head-chopper-off-er* to our egoic self. Her beautiful black body of mysteries is waiting to be explored by higher aspects of our being (keep that in mind the next time you blow off your meditation to check e-mail or the never ending news feed).

Breaking free of the matrix (even momentarily), and mastering the mind, requires a fierce commitment to our practice. We need to use laser-sharp focus to cut through all the static. Otherwise, we find ourselves right back in the realm of the ego, the time bound self, and the mind, getting buffeted and knocked around again.

The mind and ego will relentlessly hijack your awareness until you learn to master them. Mastery means you reach a point where you have the choice – and you make that choice, moment by moment – to create space between your true self (the silent observer) and the perpetual thoughts and insanely convincing projections of the ego and the mind (the matrix).

With daily practice you will move along rather quickly. Soon you will be able to access your deeper presence more-or-less whenever you want to. You will find your access point, I say, before thirty days is up. After that, you are going to stay with your unbound/timeless self for longer and longer spans of time in your meditation. You will start enjoying the indescribable peace, in your meditation, of floating in the empty spaces between your thoughts. In my experience, even if you only connect to the field of pure awareness for a few moments at a time, it is enough. With practice, comes the ability to stay with that experience for longer and longer periods of time. Those moments will evolve exponentially, kaleidoscopically, into more encompassing moments. You will begin to have new insights about yourself, and be able to respond to life, rather than only reacting to life - as before.

At the very core of your being exists the greatest power and the greatest intelligence in the universe. As Anand says, just accept this as a fact. The moment you accept this as a fact, you are awake. This presence longs for your attention, and when you give it, you will merge with it. Once you internally find your access point to the field of pure awareness, you can begin to bring this connection – this presence – out of your meditation sessions, and into the rest of your day.

This is called practicing split awareness or split attention. It is not a complicated practice, it is not a great secret, but it does require commitment because we are so deeply conditioned to live only in time, only in the realm of mind. It is so addicting and so unbelievably easy to let mind and ego be in charge of every moment. Don't let the simplicity of this practice fool you into dismissing its power. Again, mind and ego love to overcomplicate things.

You will have to work very hard against the prevailing currents in your mind until the patterns of convenience begin to break apart. As you go about your day, periodically stop what you are doing and pull part of your awareness back. As you pull part of your attention back, let that part reconnect with the *presence* you are cultivating a connection with in your meditation. Take a deep breath and simply feel into that presence again. I sometimes picture a thumb size flame just behind the base of my skull and I breathe into that power source. Use imagery that works for you. Then simply go forward with whatever you were doing. It only takes a few moments. Practice this as much as you can in your daily life and observe how it changes your experience. The more I play around with having a split awareness, the better I feel that day. It seems to bring a sense of ease, enjoyment, and playfulness back into my everyday life. Everything I look at from this split awareness appears slightly more vibrant, and I am filled with a sense of calm and well-being. It makes me feel like I have a big smile on the inside.

Eventually, with practice and time, this great silent presence will become more integrated into your self. Your body will become more attuned to the music of the universe, and able to carry that tune more and more into your daily life. When you are feeling "off," you will notice it more quickly and feel the need to get back into sync with yourself. Soon you will no longer need to look within. Within and without will merge, and you become what Anand calls a "warrior of wisdom," or what is also called an "awakened being." Anyone with a normally functioning brain can become an awakened being. It is not something far away only happening to gurus in caves in the Himalayas. It happens to everyday people in everyday lives with bunions and car payments and regular jobs. When you encounter an awakened being, you will notice a gentle confidence, a powerful calm, and an unusual clarity. You will feel a softness, a kindness, and a deep strength in their company. They do not need to tell you how powerful they are, they just are powerful. That power resides in you too, although it may be deeply asleep. You only need to connect to source, to God, to the silent observer, call it whatever you like. Imagine this presence however you like. Just do whatever you have to do to stay connected to it as much as possible. The world could probably use as many awakened beings as possible right about now.

Chapter 10

Oh The Things You'll See:
Freedom on All Levels

*"You arrive in this world with fists clinched, brow furrowed,
and you are crying while everyone else is laughing – live
your life so that when you leave this world, you go
with palms open, face smiling, and you are
laughing while everyone else is crying."*
–Hindu Proverb

The invitation to enjoy freedom on all levels is an invitation to experience yourself as the limitless, unbounded self, expressing itself playfully within the constraints of the spacetime continuum. We have the choice to reside as consciousness itself, rather than only as the content of consciousness. The content of your mind is not you. The suggestion is to unhook our awareness from the matrix of fear, incessant thought, and stories about the past and future as much as possible. We do this through technique. It is probably too much to ask of ourselves to never be afraid or have anxiety. It is enough to try to have just a little more trust than fear.

Yogic traditions offer effective technique and practices for our time, such as the ones I have shared with you. In Autobiography of a Yogi, Majavatar Babaji predicted that eastern yogic practices would reach across to the western world and the blending of east and west would offer healing and balance to the world. He said this, "The Kriya Yoga that I am giving to the world through you in this nineteenth century is a revival of the same science that Krishna gave millenniums ago to Arjuna; and that was later known to Patanjali and Christ, and to St. John, St. Paul, and other disciples." Whether you use these, or you find tools elsewhere, pick up some tools and use them. Our tendency to identify only with the content of our minds creates a form of slavery. In this state, we experience mostly bondage, conflict, and waiting. We think we are free but when we live only in the time-bound self, we are simply a product of our culture, conditioning, our story, our desires, and our fears. We only experience the storms and waves on the surface, while a calm, deep, and mysterious world awaits, unexplored.

The gifts we can receive from awakening are priceless. Here are a few of the attributes of an awakened being, according to Anand and his lineage of great teachers:

- Experience a continuity in their inner world, and are less affected by the constant fluctuations on the surfaces of the small mind.
- The awakened being is highly observant, self-reflecting, powerful beyond thought, but innocent and humble.
- Fierce in his or her wisdom, yet supremely gentle and compassionate (non-judgmental)
- Spontaneous, sincere, and playful, with a clear sense of direction.
- Deeply rooted in a timeless presence – who was never born and never dies – yet living also in the time-bound self, and intensely aware of the limitations as such.
- Self-confident, yet absolutely willing to listen, learn, and refine oneself.
- Able to love fully, but without earthly attachment or illusion.

- Able to participate fully in the play of time (the Matrix/ Maya), yet aware of the transient nature of this play.

This is how we can start to master and to beat the levels of Earthgame. Free yourself from the puppetry at the hands of ego and the mind. Play the game fearlessly whenever possible; stay in your body as much as possible; spend time with the timeless self. Use the power of free will to accept your emotions, master the ego, and explore higher levels. Remember that life is experiencing herself through you, and you ARE her. Merge with life moment to moment by totally accepting her on her terms. Keep in mind that even as we play higher levels of Earthgame, we are not going to be perfect. We will fall out of tune, and experience the full spectrum of emotions, and make all kinds of mistakes. We are human, we will never be perfect, but if we try, freedom (Nirvana, Brahman, the field of pure consciousness, whatever you want to call it) is available to us here, eternally, in each perfectly unfolding moment.

Good Luck, Gamers!

ROCHELLE P. BARTHOLOMEW

Earthgame: Hints on Mastering the Greatest Game in the Universe

CPSIA information can be obtained
at www.ICGtesting.com
Printed in the USA
FSOW01n2130200617
35460FS